DEAR VOICE

SPEAK

BY JENNIFER MOJICA ACADEMIA

Copyright © 2022 Jennifer Academia
Academia Press Publishing

ISBN: 978-1-7354007-4-7 Hard Copy
       978-1-7354007-5-4 eBook

www.jennifermojicaacademia.com

Library of Congress Control Number: 2022903642

All rights reserved.

No part of this book may be reproduced or transmitted in any form or by any means without written permission from the author. For permission, contact the Author, Jennifer Mojica Academia at JMojicaAcademia@gmail.com.

Editor - www.tiffanyvakilian.com

Logo - www.michaelkhamodesign.com

Cover and Illustrations - www.rianneelyse.myportfolio.com

PREFACE

I wrote this book to break the barriers that not only silenced my voice but for so many others who have been silenced from the sexual trauma they've endured.

Listen, the pain from trauma *always* finds a way to express itself.

It breaks all family, religious, generational, cultural, colonial, and systemic rules. I found that it is in the breaking of these rules where you will find yourself immersed in the realm of healing. It is in this realm you will find your inner strength and your unique sound. As I create this multi-dimensional space for you to heal, my hope is that you give yourself permission to open up. As you read my words, find your voice and speak your own truth about uninvited experiences with trauma.

It's time.

YOU ARE FREE FROM EVERY NEGATIVE EMOTION:
ANGER, SADNESS, FEAR, HURT, and GUILT...

Author's Note

I write so I won't hurt.

    I write to release my deepest, raw, feelings that you cannot speak. I write so you won't hurt. I write because I carry your voice in every word *I* say. I write for someone that needs to be validated. I write for someone that needs to be *seen*. I write for someone who needs her "silent scream" to be heard.
    And I am not alone. We write.
    We write to give hope to the hopeless and a voice to the voiceless. We write not only for the women in my culture, but for those who were unwillingly, immersed into a culture of sexual oppression.
    Dear voice, speak.

There may be moments while you read these collection of poems, emotional wounds may be triggered.
You are not alone.
If you need immediate help or just someone to talk to, The National Sexual Assault Hotline is also available 24 hours at 1-800-656-4673. The National Suicide Prevention Lifeline is available 24/7 at 1-800-273-8255. You can also reach out for help by texting the word HOME to 741741.
Trained volunteers can talk to you, guide you, and create a plan to help you feel a sense of calmness and safety. You matter tremendously to me, and you are worth taking the journey towards your complete healing.

FOREWORD

Every woman has heard these words: behave, smile, keep a secret, stop being a bitch, obey. For a woman to let you in, she must feel safe, seen, and understood. With that level of vulnerability, must come trust. Trust that can ultimately be broken.

In her debut book of poetry, *Dear Voice: Speak*, Jennifer Mojica-Academia shares with the reader her most honest moments, though not always pleasant, opening years of buried pain until there is nothing left to do but to speak.

Jen takes a hard look at herself in poems such as "My Complete Sentence," "Starving to Be Free," and "I Am More Than a Vagina," where she is "poked, slammed, banged, stretched, bruised and bit." Jen does not propose a solution to her pain, but rather a release through writing, as only a true artist can describe. The cries of a sad girl have become tears of healing for Jen.

A woman will lose her self-worth for a man and somehow perceive that as an act of love. And with so much guilt built up, she believes she deserves it, the molestation, the rape, the shame, the hate. No really means Yes! Have your way with her. Do as you please to her body. A fist to her head. A finger between her legs. It was all her fault. Jen believed she was to blame.

It is said that if you fall seven times, you must get up eight. But what if you can't. You just collapse to your knees with your hands covering your face, and you stay there. You wonder if anyone loves you, including yourself. Then you realize maybe defeat is necessary to move forward.

Being fearful but telling your story is the true definition of courage. Jen is courageous, even during what appears to be her weakest moments. Toni Morrison, Maya Angelou, and bell hooks all spoke with truth. We can add Jen to that list. She earned it.

To Jen's reader, you, too, are brave. You are a part of *Dear Voice: Speak*. Let's rejoice in Jen's words, as women, together we will continue to exist.

Jen is resilient, will no longer stay quiet, will no longer keep a secret. Her hurt is our hurt. Her healing is our healing. She connects us to the human experience of what it feels like to find love in ourselves again:

It's not too late.
For Jen is here.
She never left.

Veracruz Sanchez
Award-winning Author
San Diego, CA
March 2022

DEDICATION

This book is dedicated to the voiceless and to the defenseless.

TABLE OF CONTENTS

Preface i
Author's Note iii
Foreword iv
Dedication vi
    Bonedust 1
    Faces 4
    Fragmented 5
    Alone 6
    Later 6
    Floating 7
    Night Shift 8
    Disappeared 9
    Mirror, Mirror 10
    The Residue 11
    No Name 13
    The Cost of the Binge 14
    Diagnosed 15
    Without the Weight 16
    Exhausted 17
    Starving To Be Free 19
    Still 21
    Desensitized 21

- This Day 22
- NEVER 23
- I Am More Than a Vagina 25
- I am More Than a Vagina No. 2 26
- My Complete Sentence 26
- Respect The Vagina 27
- False Protection 28
- Me and Them 29
- For Charlene 30
- The Other Side of It 32
- This Before That 32
- Perfection 33
- Twisted 35
- Dear Voice, ... 36
- In Unison 39
- Breathe 40
- After Then 41

About the Author 43

DEAR VOICE

SPEAK

BONEDUST

From a dream that I have had since I was 9 years old:

I was in my mom and dad's backyard
Arrested by fear and disgust as I saw myself excavating multiple tombs
tormented by what people will assume.

Next
I saw myself in mom and dad's garage with eight Hefty Glad trash bags
How sad!
eight
the number of "New Beginnings"
So I thought, *this can't be all that bad.*

Inside each bag
human remains
some were new
some were fragile and
some appeared ancient

I still was not sure what all this meant

As the garage door opened
slightly
allowing sunlight in
I squatted behind the bags
hiding
out of fear of being accused.

I saw myself holding a large hammer
Grasping it with my right hand
glowing
growing
larger than the rest of me
obviously

Dear Voice

I was under His command.

Then
one by one
each bone was pulverized
by this hammer in my right hand
larger than me
pulverized to dust

I heard the sound of a strong wind approaching
likened to the sound of God
the night before He prepared the parting of the Red Sea
Am I to play a part in delivering
His men,
women and children
Free?
Yes
FREE!

The strength of the wind blew the dust away
Away
in the four directions
North, South, East and West.

The Wind speaks:
I chose you, because you are clearly my best
pulverize generations after generations
of sexual perversity and
emotion unrest

One by one
each bone
pulverized
by this hammer
by my right hand
larger than me
pulverized to dust

This recurring dream finally stopped after mama died: 11/21/15

FACES

Putting on the many faces of a lie takes a lot of prep
living in a soul
dark, empty, and without depth
Will they like me with this face or will they like me with that face
Dreading the time of ultimately being replaced
Academy award for best actress
night after night
until you are no longer recognizable
to your own self

Fragmented

He took away my innocence

I slowly aligned myself with how my pain defined me

Addict

    Drinker

                                  Cutter

                                                    Suicidal

                              Actress

    Whore

Fragmented to the core

ALONE

How can someone feel so alone around so many people
The isolation
The deafening sound
I wanted to scream
But I was silenced

                Until now…

LATER

I see my brother and sister's baby picture on the family room wall.
My picture isn't there.
I ask her, "Where's my picture?"
She explains, "I am still looking for the right one
and will hang your picture up *later.*"
5 years came.
10 years came.
25 years came.
Her death came.
Later
Never
Came

FLOATING

I see me
I see what you are doing to me from afar
No longer feeling
No more sound
No longer moving

Only   Ceiling

Floating   The

Into   Into

The ceiling   Floating

Only

I see me
I see what you are doing to me from afar
No longer feeling
No more sound
No longer moving

Night Shift

When our eyes met
I knew "for sure" he was it.
I cooked every meal
and quickly learned what he likes to feel
I submitted to all of his needs
In return, hurt and pain received
The passionate evenings were on the decline
the kind exchange of words was a struggle to find
Soon he claimed that he was bored
Yet refused to let me move forward
How is it that my "for sure" feels like number 8?
Or was it number 9?
No.
It was number 10
The "loser after loser" syndrome strikes again!
Different person, same loser. When will I get it right?
When will I choose to stop bringing home the same fools, night after night?!
Since when do I need permission to live my life?
It's time to cut the soul ties and reconcile with my inner strife.

Disappeared

With each year
a part of me disappeared
each hurtful word from her lips
cut like a knife

With each decade
a part of me disappeared
her countenance of disgust and disappointment
faded my inner beauty

With the passage of time
a part of me disappeared
into the wall
each time my safety was breached

With the time that crept by
a part of me disappeared
buried in darkness
as death constantly seduced me.

Time slipped by
parts of me disappeared
taken away
some given away
for my value never existed in her eyes.

I

never existed

in her eyes.

Mirror, Mirror

"Yes, I know what was happening to you," was my brother's reply.
"You were like a video playing that no one watched."

My family pretended that it never took place
I was swept under the rug
no trace
But I knew how pretention would resurface in my face
And in the face
of others
projecting reasons for what happened IN me, and not to me,
Recovery, doubtful daily
Was it fear
Was it shame
Could what happened to me embarrass the family name
Was it our culture
Was it the fact
that the responsibility
for not protecting me
was the reality

Or was what happened to me
what happened to you

Now all the emotions
denied all these years
no longer dormant
still, silenced truth

Mirror, Mirror
when you look at me,

you see you

The Residue

It sticks like glue and unexpectedly hits me
    when it's just you and I, intimately
    My mind can't stay present as my body feels
    tangibly
    it's for rent
    again

Wanting to authentically respond to you
    not just pretend
    I softly smile as your faithfulness brings my soul renewal

Yet
    I fight, flight, or freeze as my heart and mind play
    Shot for shot
    an all-out bloody duel

How long will you tolerate my mental torment?
Can you just hold me as my body laments?
It's not about you, though you must feel the torrent.

I just needed you to know
That
One day
    I will believe you when you say I am beautiful
One day
    I will receive every dimension of who you are

Without fear
Without the internal voices
Just me
Presenting all
Giving my whole self to you

Dear Voice

No Name

Empty
Deep
Deep
Deep
Inside

Yet

so FULL of emotions.

The Cost of the Binge

The loss of money
The loss of peace
The loss of feeling alive
A unique kind of grief
As if someone
Died

The loss of innocence
The loss of hope
The loss of creativity
my entire of essence

I was so young
and nothing made sense
Participating
out of fear

The loss left a weight in my chest
a deep pit in my stomach

Diagnosed

When the intent
was sent
for my entirety to be humiliated
grief
loss
impulsive eating
purging
and self-starvation
consummated

I ate
and I ate
impulsively
dangerously
diagnosed
"severe"
DIET Programs and calorie restriction
a toxic career

WITHOUT THE WEIGHT

Without the weight
The real me was stolen
I needed to feel the gravity
the weight
of my existence

Without the weight
I was afraid I would forget
I didn't want to
forget who I was
forget how I was creative
forget how I mattered
forget the brief sound
my belly
aching with laugher
not hunger

EXHAUSTED

The binges and purges persisted
throughout the decades
The pressure
The shame
The guilt
The excessive exercise to punish myself
The food obsessions
The laxatives
The mental exhaustion
The unclean motives
The secrets
The lies
Oh, the vanity
Vying to meet American beauty standards
Just insanity
my entire body
stuffed with a dozen hand grenades

"Am I going to pull out the pins
right now?"

Why not?"

After a tub of ice cream
And a half a cake
I felt it
I believed it
I was a big, fat cow!
Should I eat this or not
cognitive dissonance
deafening my mind

as I grow in size

Dear Voice

I become hyper-visible
no place to hide

I wonder
are the voices in my head
now audible
to the outside?
My body obeys the vibrations
The deep groans in my soul
my flesh fades away
in the least restrictive flow

Dead fish go with the flow, too

Starving To Be Free

I push my food to different parts of my plate
My mind
slowly filled
with self-hate
It's easy to not eat
it's easier to get rid of it
It's an accepted method of annihilating the shame
bit by bit
I have convinced my body
that anything entering
anything inside it
CANNOT stay,
must come out
Does anyone out there, even know what I'm fucking talking about??

It's almost exhilarating
controlling my appetite
But I still find myself struggling
the fear of him
entering
the fear of him
inside me
during the night
just maybe
he won't disturb me

Perhaps if I don't grow any hips
any breast
Prayerfully

Dear Voice

What I thought I had control over
had control over me
No matter how much I tried to stop him,
He kept breaking me
wouldn't stop taking my parts
Leaving me bruised, sore
Even when there wasn't much left of me
his appetite for me
agonizing and insatiable

STILL

I used every method to numb my feelings
Completely deprived from the power of all sensations
Insidiously, pain still finds a way to ambush me

DESENSITIZED

Repeated exposure of shocking views
It keeps you from feeling what is intuitively true
Desensitized

A fading history
Tolerant of everything auditory and visually
Desensitized

Accepting the new
"Don't even think for yourself" is the blatant mandate
Or
risk being accused as full of hate

An attempt to keep me dull and imprisoned for my choice
Venomously, too silent my voice
Desensitized

I refuse to negotiate
my beliefs and values and to keep the faith
Desensitized

THIS DAY

It is this day that I hold you for the very first time
Tears stream down my face
Your name, Graceful, was an unconscious decision to erase
The shame that came
When I became my family's disgrace
It is this day that you are finally born
so beautiful
so pure
so innocent
so fragile
so helpless and unable to defend
You are me redeemed
Your existence became the start of making amends
from within
You are solely dependent on me
Your mother,
To protect you
To love you
To cherish and care for you
It is this day, that I understand
I am not to blame.
I, too, was only a child.

I was only a child.

11/21/1992

NEVER

I never agreed to smell you up close

I never agreed to touch you

I never agreed for you to touch me

I never agreed for you to threaten me

I never agreed to be raped by you

This was never "our little secret".

Dear Voice

I Am More Than a Vagina

I am more than a vagina
I said,
Read my lips
I do more than provide a place of pleasure
I do more than take an unquenchable pounding

It's from this place I have the power to create
It's from this place you wish to donate
It's from this place I write as a scribe
It's from this same place you negotiate a bribe
It's from this place I discover a melody
It's from this same place you force yourself on me, eventually

You think you can control, own, and destroy me
I've got news for you
This Vagina of mine was miraculously created by Eternity

I am more than a Vagina
I am not a commodity
Read my LIPS
I am beauty…
I am wise…
I am courage…
I am strength…
I am present…
I am SEEN…
I am valuable…
I matter…

this is my brand-new start
I am a powerful woman with who has forgiven herself and others with the totality of her heart.

I am More Than a Vagina No. 2

Truly resilient
This vagina of mine
Poked, slammed, banged, stretched, bruised and bit
Trust me, this powerful vagina of mine, took on a lot of sh-t!

I am the final stop before the birth
Yet the starting point of the removal of my skirt

I am more than a delicious "part"
The rest of me is a beautiful work of art

My Complete Sentence

The power of
a short
complete
sentence
Hear me now.
I said it then, too.

"NO."

Respect The Vagina

Two breast that nurture and care
Big or small, they draw your stare

A behind to squeeze, admire, and slap
And ohhhhhh, how you crave me bouncing on your lap

A neck to see dripping with sweat

The power of the vagina when swelled and wet
Impatience grows as you long for the next time you can get

Two eyes that can stare deep and hypnotize
But all you can think of is my creamy, voluptuous thighs

A mouth that can speak power and intensity
While demanding sincerity, eternity, and integrity

Yet entering its soft, moist flesh
can send you off to ecstasy

Two legs that can strap, stretch, and bend
You are amazed with how far they can extend

Two hands that can strategically stroke and caress
They start and stop you and place you under pleasurable duress

A nose to smell pheromones or to detect
Never forget,
> **every part of me deserves your respect**

FALSE PROTECTION

Unforgiveness
 doesn't
 protect you

Unforgiveness
doesn't
prevent you
from getting hurt

They
The unforgiven
don't even know
They
Those you hold
don't even care

You are suffering

Forgive them

For yourself

Me and Them

There is no DNA
To validate the truth in what I say

All I know was, without a word, I represented disgrace
Tormented with shame, I lived like a misfit and displaced
This pain consumes my breath and entire space

I look in every direction
Obsessing over what they see as perfection

My family tells me,
"Don't say a word"
"Just move on"
"Be strong"

Little did they know that what I needed was to be free of this pain, and simply belong

Living a life as though the abuse never happened
is the ultimate self-betrayal
with multiple replays of the abuse
and feeling abandoned

No longer will I participate in these manipulations
Telling the truth will not only save me
It is freeing the next generations

Dear Voice

For Charlene

She saw me for the first time
And spoke to me
I couldn't receive what she perceived
But it was simply different
this time
I thought it was "that look"
that shook my spirit
The authority she carried
Unlocked my true identity
She spoke from a place of love
power
and truth
to a place inside me that was dry
hopeless
and needed
proof of unclean motives
when she spoke
she knew
I didn't want to live
The roots of shame, disappointment
abandonment, and betrayal
all released
if only I was willing to forgive
she saw the gifts of healing, exhortation, prophecy
all that was in me
she was called to pull me out of my complacency
to catapult me into my next place
and train me to run the race and run it well
her words melted the fortress I built
around my heart
I knew
from then on out
her words

her power
had established my new start
My heart knew her words were
not for show
How do I know?
How can I trust?
Because the voice I heard wasn't hers
It was the voice of "us"
in agreement

        I still carry her words in my spirit:
    "You are so beautiful and Powerful!

THE OTHER SIDE OF IT

Sometimes I hurt because of what you didn't say
Sometimes I hurt because of what you didn't do
Sometimes I hurt because of your disapproval for me desiring something new

Sometimes I hurt because you didn't have the capacity
to love me the way I needed you to love me

I forgive you.

THIS BEFORE THAT

You must be sifted before you are shifted
You must give mercy before you receive it
You must be willing to forgive before bitterness takes root
You must know how to say no before you can clearly see your yes
You must pause before you respond
You must stay low before you go high
You must respect time before it runs out
You must grieve before you can truly love

Perfection

Perfection is the insurrection that grabs hold and poisons our soul
It fights against our own authority, contending for complete control

I've accepted that I am the minority
Not just my skin color but by design and purpose
Something powerful took place from within
Once I chose to remove myself from Deception's circus

Releasing the striving
created out of distortion
From victim to victor
I have claimed my portion

Overpowered the mess, stress, and duress
And put the impact of the trauma under complete arrest
This is truly the best, I can attest

To be at peace in mind, body, and spirit

To walk in excellence, unbound by anyone's preference

Enables me to stomp on microaggression, biases- cultural, implicit and explicit

It's through seasons of studying the darkness
I've discovered self-love and self-compassion

It's through engaging my quest for perfection
God found me imperfect, and set me perfectly free

Dear Voice

Twisted

Why do you think that the person who broke you
is the same person that can heal you

Stop waiting

The apology isn't coming

Dear Voice,

No one listened to you.
No one believed you.

So, *Lying Voice* showed up to help teach you the way to get attention.

Lying Voice slowly became louder and more convincing compared to *Honest Voice*, the "Honorable Mention."

Lying Voice became a way of safety.
Lying Voice became a way to be seen.
Lying Voice became a way of survival, not like every teen.

"I am fine," say's *Lying Voice*, when deep down inside, she wanted to die.

"I like it," says *Lying Voice*, just to make him finish faster. Even now, she cries.

Lying Voice grew stronger when she discovered that she became a way of making sense
when the truth was too painful.

Honest Voice says to *Lying Voice*, "Stop making promises to yourself and to others that you can't keep.
That's not faithful.
That's so unacceptable.
How dare you, *Lying Voice*, you hypocrite!"
She doesn't even throw a fit!

Lying Voice, you have many faces:
    You look like fear.
    You look like survival.
    You look like control.

You look like manipulation.
You look like shame.
You look like love.
You look like strength.
You look smart and dread the next time the acting must start again.
You look like seduction.
You look like deception.
You cringe with the anxiety of a confirmed conception.

Lying Voice, today I am listening to your voice
and I cry for your many faces.
I hear YOUR VOICE of pain for being with so many races.

I hear YOUR VOICE of trauma.
I hear YOUR VOICE of fear.
I hear YOUR VOICE whimpering tears. Wishing someone was near.

I hear YOUR VOICE of exhaustion from all of your endless attempts of creating love,
when all this led to was washing off their filth in your tub.

Lying Voice says to herself, "It's soft porn; it's not that bad,"
as she robotically begins to blow his horn.

I hear YOUR *DESPERATE* VOICE for safety and protection,
but all you received were *multiple* erections.

I hear YOUR VOICE of needing to be held without anyone sticking their tongue down
your throat.

I hear YOUR VOICE of yearning to feel beautiful and cherished without paying the
price of the unwanted thrusting, so you "float" into the ceiling.

I hear YOUR VOICE screaming "NO MORE!" as no one listened.

You were heard, but no one listened.

I hear YOUR VOICE as you witness "justice" fall.
Lying Voice, you mastered you so well that you convinced yourself to believe that you
ARE truth.
OH, the irony of it all!!!

Honest Voice asked herself, "How do I un-create this counterfeit voice when the root
of its very purpose was created from the pure desperation
of telling the truth and for the
courts to file, yet she was only met with her mother's inscrutable piercing
countenance of cultural denial?"

Honest Voice asks herself, "How do I gracefully shut the door of
this lying voice that
was opened by a desecrated, 12-year-old little girl?"

Dear *Lying Voice*,
You've aged out.
 I see you.
 I hear you.
 I honor you.
You are safe now.
You can go now.
Thank you for your service.

Sincerely,
Honest Voice

In Unison

I walked towards her body with my brother and sister
for strength
to close
our mother's casket
one last time.

I felt the weight of the lid.
I watched her face
slowly disappear
as the cover was descending.

The coffin finally slammed shut.

As I walked back to my seat,
slowly,
the sleeping part of my soul began to quiver
louder and louder, and

without permission
suddenly
I felt the dams of my wells
burst forth.

At that very moment
I felt
a colossal,
magnetic force
pulling in
all of the fragmented wounded pieces
parts of what once defined me.

As the casket lid slammed shut,
each wounded fragment gathered together for the first time

Dear Voice

In a long time
In UNISON

I released a ***DEEP***
Echoing

      Heart Piercing

           Primordial

              Vibrational

SOUND

BREATHE

Finally, I can inhale (*Alo*) and exhale (*HAAAAAAAAA*)

    Quietly

    Deeply

    Freely
    And
        Completely

AFTER THEN
Dedicated to my Ride or Die

Even when I was frozen
Even after the lies
Even after the weight gain
Even after threats
Even after I told you all my regrets
Even after cussing
Even after the losses
Even after brokenness
Even after tears
Even after the hurtful words
Even after all the screaming
Even after withholding myself

You whisper to me,
"I'm still here."

YOU ARE FREE FROM EVERY NEGATIVE EMOTION:
ANGER, SADNESS, FEAR, HURT, and GUILT...

About the Author

Jennifer Mojica-Academia has served as an educator and mental health professional for over two decades. She was born and raised in San Diego and has been married to her husband, Paul, for over 20 years. Jennifer graduated from UCSD with a B.A. in Psychology and minored in African American Music. She also graduated from SDSU with an M.S. in Marriage and Family Counseling. She completed her Pupil Personnel Services Credential from National University and her Administrative Credential from Point Loma Nazarene University.

She has also received her Certifications as a Practitioner in Neurolinguistic Programming, Time Line Therapy, and Hypnotherapy.

Her heart is to serve, loving people through to their best, deepest, most intimate purpose and callings. She has answered the call to encourage and speak life into the lives of women overcoming trauma.

This is the first time she's spoken openly about her own story.

www.jennifermojicaacademia.com
Instagram - @JenMojicaAcademia
IO Podcast Interview

CPSIA information can be obtained
at www.ICGtesting.com
Printed in the USA
BVHW091535090522
636525BV00028B/351